Level 2 is ideal for children who have rec... some reading instruction and c... simple sentences with help.

Special features:

Frequent repetition of main story words and phrases

Short, simple sentences

Green and his family lived in a monster house.

They had monster baths and monster dinners.

Large, clear type

"I wish I was a monster," said George.

"I wish I was an ordinary boy," said Green. So...

George went to live at Green's house next door. Green went to live at George's house.

Careful match between story and pictures

Educational Consultant: Geraldine Taylor
Book Banding Consultant: Kate Ruttle

LADYBIRD BOOKS

UK | USA | Canada | Ireland | Australia
India | New Zealand | South Africa

Ladybird Books is part of the Penguin Random House group of companies
whose addresses can be found at global.penguinrandomhouse.com.

ladybird.com

Penguin
Random House
UK

First published 2015
001

Ladybird, Read it yourself and the Ladybird logo are registered or
unregistered trademarks owned by Ladybird Books Ltd

The moral right of the author and illustrator has been asserted

Printed in China

A CIP catalogue record for this book is available from the British Library

ISBN: 978–0–723–29524–2

The Monster
Next Door

Written by Mandy Ross
Illustrated by Gavin Scott

George was an ordinary boy,
with an ordinary family.

Green was a monster,
with a monster family.

George lived next door
to Green.

Green and his family lived in a monster house.

They had monster baths and monster dinners.

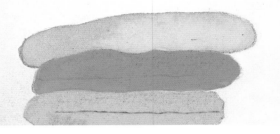

9

George and his family lived in an ordinary house.

They had ordinary baths and ordinary dinners.

Green played monster games.

"I wish I could play monster games," said George.

George played ordinary games.

"I wish I could play ordinary games," said Green.

13

"I wish I was a monster," said George.

"I wish I was an ordinary boy," said Green. So...

George went to live at Green's house next door. Green went to live at George's house.

15

"Hello!" said George's mum.
"Come in. It is dinner time."

"Hello!" said Green's dad.
"Come in! It is dinner time."

"This is our favourite dinner," said Green's dad. "Tasty green slime."

"Green slime?" said George. "Oh no! I can't eat that!"

19

"This is our favourite dinner," said George's mum. "Tasty fish and chips."

"Fish and chips?" said Green. "Oh no! I can't eat that!"

Then it was time for a bath at the monsters' house.

"Jump in the bath!" said Green's dad. "Time to get clean."

"Oh no!" said George. "Not in a bath of slime!"

It was time for a bath at George's house, too.

"Jump in the water!" said George's mum. "Time to get clean."

"Oh no!" said Green. "Not in a bath of water!"

Then it was time for bed.

"Oh no!" said George.
"Not in a bed of slime!"

"Oh no!" said Green.
"Not in a clean bed!"

So George ran back
home and Green ran
back home, too.

"I am glad I am a monster,"
said Green.

"I am glad I am an ordinary
boy," said George.

How much do you remember about the story of The Monster Next Door? Answer these questions and find out!

- Who lives in an ordinary house?

- Who has tasty green slime for dinner?

- Who does not want to eat fish and chips?

- What do George and Green do at the end of the story?

Look at the pictures and match them to the story words.

George

Green

slime

fish and chips

bed

Tick the books you've read!

Level 2

Level 3